MW01045123

Lady with the Lamp

The Florence Nightingale Story

By Alan Trussell-Cullen

Illustrated by Mike Lacey

⌐ Dominie Press, Inc.

Publisher: Raymond Yuen
Project Editor: John S. F. Graham
Editor: Bob Rowland
Designer: Greg DiGenti
Illustrator: Mike Lacey

Published by:

꘎ Dominie Press, Inc.

1949 Kellogg Avenue
Carlsbad, California 92008 USA

www.dominie.com

1-800-232-4570

Paperback ISBN 0-7685-1824-5
Printed in Singapore by PH Productions Pte Ltd
1 2 3 4 5 6 PH 05 04 03

Table of Contents

Chapter One

A Girl with Nothing to Do

On May 12, 1820, an Englishwoman gave birth to a little girl in the beautiful city of Florence, Italy. The woman and her husband thought their baby daughter was as beautiful as the city itself, so they named her Florence—Florence Nightingale.

Florence's parents were very rich. As Florence grew up in London, her family was able to give her everything she needed. Her mother expected her to do what other rich English girls did— they were expected to visit friends and go to parties and eventually marry a rich young man. Rich girls certainly weren't expected to work or have jobs.

But Florence wasn't like the other rich girls. At sixteen, she decided she wanted to spend her life doing things to help others. There were many sick people who lived near their home in England. Florence started visiting sick people and bringing them food and medicine.

Her parents thought this was all right, but when she asked if she could go to learn how to be a nurse at a nearby hospital, they were horrified. Hospitals in

those days were crowded places. They were dirty and smelly. The nurses who worked there were poorly educated and knew very little about caring for people. Florence's parents didn't want her to be around those kinds of people.

But what was even more shocking for Florence's parents was the idea that their daughter wanted to *work*! Rich girls didn't have jobs in those days.

Her family sent Florence on a trip to Europe to try to make her forget these ideas. But this only made Florence all the more determined to become a nurse.

While traveling through Germany, she visited the Kaiserwerth Institute, which had a good hospital and was one of the few places where nurses could be trained. Florence went back to England and begged her father to let her go to the

Kaiserwerth Institute to study and learn to be a nurse. At first, everyone in her family was furious. But finally, in 1851, her father gave in.

Chapter Two
A Nurse at Last

All the people at the Kaiserwerth Institute had devoted their lives to helping others. There was a hospital for sick people, schools, and an orphanage for homeless children. The work was very hard. Florence had to get up each morning at five o'clock, and she worked all day and long into the night. But she loved it.

"I am as happy as the day is long!" she wrote in her diary.

After her training, Florence returned to London, where she was determined to put her nurse's training to work. She took charge of nursing at a number of hospitals. But in 1854 there was an outbreak of cholera. This terrible disease is very easy to catch, and it spreads very quickly. In those days, many people died of cholera. The nearby Middlesex Hospital was full of people who were sick and dying of the disease. Florence didn't hesitate. She took charge of the hospital and did everything she could for the patients.

It was good training for what was to be the next and greatest challenge of her life.

Chapter Three
War Breaks Out

In March, 1854, war broke out in Crimea between Russia and Turkey. A year later, Britain and France joined Turkey in the battle against the Russians. But the war went badly, and soon there were many sick and wounded soldiers.

They were taken to a hospital in Scutari, Turkey.

Conditions in the hospital were appalling. There were no nurses to help the doctors. The doctors were not only trying to help the soldiers who had been wounded in battle, but they were also doing what they could for soldiers who were sick and dying of terrible diseases like cholera and typhus. Five out of every six soldiers who died in the Scutari Hospital died of these diseases rather than their battle wounds.

"This is not right!" thundered Florence, when she read in the newspapers about the suffering of the soldiers in Crimea. She sat down to write a letter to Sir Sidney Herbert, an old friend in the government. She offered to take charge of the nursing in Crimea.

14

At exactly the same time, Sir Sidney was writing a letter to *her*, begging her to come and help!

Florence sprang into action. She quickly gathered a group of 38 nurses and set sail for Scutari.

When she arrived, she was horrified. The hospital was filthy. There was hardly any clean water, and bandages and medical supplies were scarce. Much of the food was unfit to eat. There were sick and dying soldiers everywhere, and more arrived each day. The army doctors were not able to cope.

At first, army officers and doctors resented Florence. They didn't believe women could do this kind of work. They tried to keep her and her nurses out of the hospital.

"How could a group of women possibly

help here? Just go home to England and do your embroidery!" they said.

"We'll wait for you to change your mind," said Florence. And they waited.

More and more sick and wounded soldiers began to arrive in the already overcrowded hospital. Finally, the army officers and doctors turned to Florence.

"Please, will you help?" they said.

Immediately, Florence and her team went to work. Florence had noticed that fewer people died in hospitals when conditions were cleaner and there was fresh water available.

They brought fresh water in and cleaned the hospital from top to bottom. They nursed the patients and dressed their wounds. Fewer soldiers caught diseases like dysentery, cholera, and typhus, which spread easily. Florence and her nurses washed all the clothing and bedding. They cooked good food to help the sick recover. They worked tirelessly.

Florence hardly had any time to sleep. She wrote letters home for the soldiers who couldn't write, and at night she walked through every ward of the hospital. She carried a lamp with her, and she said goodnight to every single person. The soldiers came to love her. They called her the Lady with the Lamp.

In those days, news traveled very slowly. But in time, word of Florence's work reached England, and soon the newspapers were singing the praises of Florence Nightingale and her nurses. She had become a national hero!

Chapter Four
The Nightingale Nurses

In 1856, the war in Crimea came to an end, and Florence returned to England. She was surprised to find how famous she had become. She didn't like all the fuss people were making about her.

"There is still so much that needs to be

done," she said.

Queen Victoria invited Florence to Scotland for a vacation. Florence accepted, but not because she wanted a vacation. She took the opportunity to tell the queen about all the changes that hospitals needed to make.

The queen listened carefully. Afterward, she set up a special committee to look at the way army hospitals were run. Florence was delighted. She wrote a long report for the committee, describing everything that needed to change.

But Florence wanted to change the way ordinary hospitals were run, too. "Hospitals have to be clean, well-organized, and better equipped. Nurses need to be educated and well-trained," she declared.

One of the ways Florence helped make changes was by writing letters.

She loved writing letters. She wrote to everyone she thought might help make a difference. She even wrote the first textbook for nurses, *Notes on Nursing: What It Is and What It Is Not.*

Florence continued to write letters, but her dream was to have a training school for nurses, where women could be taught how to properly take care of the sick and injured. That dream finally came true in 1860 with the establishment of the Nightingale School of Nursing, in London.

Many people gave money to help start the school, which was founded on Florence's ideas and principles. She took a personal interest in all the nurses and gave each one a gift when they finished their training.

The probationer nurses, as they were called, attended the training program for

NIGHTINGALE SCHOOL OF NURSING

a year. They dressed in plain brown uniforms and lived in a wing of Saint Thomas's Hospital, in London. All their living expenses were paid, and each received an additional allowance of £10 a year (about $50). The training for the nurses was very practical. Nurses learned how to make hospital beds, how to change dressings, and how to help doctors care for patients.

The school was to provide the foundation for the way nurses are trained, not only in England, but around the world.

Despite her fame, Florence shunned public events. She preferred to help people in a quiet way. When she returned from the Crimean War, for example, she brought back a number of homeless children and soldiers, including a one-legged sailor boy and a terribly scarred Russian soldier. Florence supported them all for the rest of her life.

The people she helped did not forget her. The city of London gave her the Freedom of the City of London award. In 1907, King Edward awarded her the Order of Merit. This is a very special award, and Florence was the first woman ever to receive it. When she died, people wanted her to be buried in Westminster Abbey alongside all the kings and queens and the country's most famous people. But in her will, Florence insisted that she be buried with her family. This famous woman, who saved thousands of lives and completely changed the way sick people are nursed and cared for around the world, remained humble and modest to the end. As she requested, all it says on her grave is: *F.N. Born 1820, Died 1910.*

The first training school for nurses in the United States was established in 1870 in Boston, and the first nurse to qualify was Linda Richards. In 1877, Linda traveled to England to continue her studies at Saint Thomas's Hospital, where she met Florence Nightingale. In time, she helped set up a number of nurse training schools in the United States and Japan.